Goldie's New Home

Written by Giles Clare

Illustrated by Maxine Lee-Mackie

Collins

One cold day, Goldie rushed home across the forest, keen to get out of the rain. But what a shock she got!

A big tree trunk had landed on her roof, flattening her house!

Then she saw the woodcutter. He was using his big chainsaw to fell lots of trees.

A poster said: New housing estate – here soon!

New
Housing Estate-
here soon!

"I cannot afford to trade my little house for a new one," said Goldie to herself. "And I cannot stay here with all these trees crashing down!"

So she set off to find a safe spot to stay.

Soon she came to a little house. It looked like no one was inside ...

But upstairs, she saw a frightening person with big teeth and a frilled nightgown! Goldie flew back downstairs and away.

Next, Goldie came to a sweet little house made of cake! It belonged to Mrs Grimm.

"Come in, my dear," grinned Mrs Grimm. "I'd like to have you for tea!"

"No thanks!" said Goldie, as she escaped.

Further on, Goldie saw an odd house made of hay.
But as she crept in, the house began to shake.

Someone outside was huffing and puffing, as if to tip the house right over! Goldie shot back out at high speed.

"This is no use," said Goldie. "What will I do?"
She looked up, and saw three squirrels making
a complicated treehouse out of twigs.

That gave Goldie an idea.

"If I cannot find a home, I can make one!"
said Goldie.

She piled up logs to make the sides of a house.
She used long twigs and fern fronds to make
a roof. The squirrels helped too!

When the house was finished, it looked amazing –
and big!

"If people need a home, they can stay here,"
said Goldie.

The next day, a little girl in a red cloak arrived. "A frightening person with big teeth has taken over my house," she said.

Then a pair of lost children came – they had escaped from Mrs Grimm!

Next, three little pigs trotted in. "Someone blew our house down!" they cried.

Homeless rabbits and weasels hopped in too.
Goldie even made a bug hotel for some
homeless insects!

Soon, Goldie's new house was full of people and living things — and full of jokes and songs, too.

"I am proud of my new home," smiled Goldie.

Goldie's poster

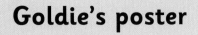

Come to
Goldie's
home!

Soft
moss
beds

Wild forest food

Fun, games and songs!

Make a bug hotel

Goldie's home hunt

❖ Review: After reading ❖

Use your assessment from hearing the children read to choose any GPCs, words or tricky words that need additional practice.

Read 1: Decoding

- Practise reading words with the new sounds. Ask the children to read these words, reminding them that the same spellings can have different sounds (e.g. *"ew" – /oo/ or /yoo/; "e" – /e/ or /ee/*).

no	he	flew	new	saw	away
these	Goldie	estate	outside	idea	

- Challenge the children to take turns to read a page aloud, but sounding out words silently. Say: Can you blend in your head when you read these words?

Read 2: Prosody

- Read page 12, modelling a storyteller voice to create suspense and drama. Point out how you used the commas and pauses to slow the story down.
- Discuss how to read page 13 to create atmosphere (e.g. *emphasising "Someone outside", building up with a tone of horror, and then using a faster pace for the action*).
- Encourage children to read pages 12 and 13 as storytellers, using your modelled reading and their own ideas.

Read 3: Comprehension

- Turn to pages 4 and 5. Discuss how the children feel about the woodcutter cutting down the trees. Do the children think it is a good or a bad idea to cut down trees to build houses? Why?
- Point to the word **trade** on page 6. Discuss what it means (e.g. *swap; sell then buy*). Ask: Why can't Goldie trade her little house for a new one? (e.g. *she hasn't got enough money*)
- Use pages 30 and 31 to prompt a discussion about each setting, what happened and the links to familiar fairy tales. Ask:
  o What happened here? What/Who links with a fairy tale? (e.g. *woodcutter, forest, wolf dressed as a grandma* – Little Red Riding Hood; *Mrs Grimm and her house* – Hansel and Gretel; *the hay house, huffing and puffing* – Three Little Pigs).
- Bonus content: On pages 28 and 29, can the children work out how to make a bug hotel just using the pictures? Ask them to make up an instruction sentence to go with each picture.